Looking at Plants

Plants and people

D0317331

Sally Morgan

BRISTOL CITY COUNCIL
LIBRARY SERVICES
WITHDRAWN AND OFFERED FOR SALE
SOLD AS SEEN

Bristol Libraries

1802359893

First published in the UK in 2002 by
Chrysalis Children's Books
An imprint of Chrysalis Books Group Plc
The Chrysalis Building, Bramley Road,
London W10 6SP

Paperback edition first published in 2004
Copyright © Chrysalis Books Group PLC 2002
Text copyright © Sally Morgan 2002

Editor: Jean Coppendale
Designer: John Jamieson
Artwork: Chris Forsey
Picture researcher: Sally Morgan
Educational consultant: Katie Kitching

All rights reserved. No part of this book may
be reproduced or utilized in any form or by
any means, electronic or mechanical, including
photocopying, recording or by any information
storage and retrieval system, without written
permission from the publisher, except by a
reviewer who may quote passages in a review.

ISBN 1 84138 433 X (Hardback)
ISBN 1 84458 136 5 (Paperback)

British Library Cataloguing in Publication Data
for this book is available from the British Library.

Printed in China / Singapore / Hong Kong

(hb)10 9 8 7 6 5 4 3 2 1
(pb)10 9 8 7 6 5 4 3 2 1

Picture acknowledgements:
E = Ecoscene, PA = Papilio, PI = Pictor
International.

Front Cover (main) & 5 E/Erik Schaffer; Title
page & 8 E/Wootton; 2 & 14 (main)
E/Gryniewicz; 3 & 26 P/Peter Worth; 4 (T) &
Cover (insets) PI/Stephen Barnett, (B) E/Amanda
Gazidis; 6 E/Alex Bartel; 7 (TL) & 30 (B) E/Peter
Currell, (TR) E/Latha Raman, (B) E/Christine
Osborne; 9 E; 10 & Cover (insets) E/Rosemary
Greenwood; 10-11 E/Anthony Cooper; 11 & 32
E/Christine Osborne; 12 (T) E/Hulme, (B)
E/Erik Schaffer; 13 E/Cooper; 14 (inset)
E/Christine Osborne; 15 (T) E, (B) E/Christine
Osborne; 16 E/Sally Morgan; 17 (T) & (C)
E/Sally Morgan, (B) & 31 E/Christine Osborne;
18 E; 19 (T) E/Christine Osborne, (B) E/Nick
Hawkes; 20 E/Gryniewicz; 21 (T) & Cover
(insets) E/Tony Page, (B) E/Sally Morgan; 22 &
Cover (insets) E/Rob Nichol; 22-23 E/Nick
Hawkes; 23 E/Mathew Bolton; 24 E/Sally
Morgan; 25 (T) E/John Farmar, (B) E/Christine
Osborne; 27 (T) E/Andrew Brown, (B) 30 (T) &
Cover (insets) E/Tony Page.

BRISTOL CITY LIBRARIES

AN1802359893

| PE | 08-Mar-2010 |
| C581.6 | £5.99 |

Contents

Words in **bold** are explained in the glossary on page 30.

Useful plants

If you look around your home you will see many different objects made from plants. Wooden furniture, newspaper, magazines, books and clothing made from cotton are just a few examples.

This cotton picker is wearing clothes made from cotton.

The paper in these books and magazines was made using wood from trees.

People need plants for food. We eat many different types of plants such as rice, wheat, fruits and vegetables. We eat the meat of animals such as cows and sheep. These animals also depend on plants, because they eat mostly grass.

A wide range of fruits and vegetables is on sale in this market in Malaysia. But many other types of plants can also be used in food.

5

Plants for food

Everybody eats plants. There are a few plants that are very important. These are the plants that give us **energy**, for example potatoes, wheat and rice. These plants are called **staple foods**. We eat them every day and they make up a large part of our **diet**.

Potato is full of starch which gives us energy. Potatoes can be boiled, roasted or fried in oil to make chips.

Rice has to be cooked before it can be eaten. It is usually boiled in water.

In many parts of the world, potatoe and wheat are the staple foods. In Asia, rice is also important. In Africa, plants such as cassava, sorghum and millet are basic foods as well.

This fully grown rice plant is ready to be harvested.

Cassava is grown in tropical places. The root of the plant is cooked and eaten.

Growing crops

Staple foods are grown in large quantities because so many people eat them. This means that the plants have to be grown as crops. **Cereal crops** grow quickly and they produce lots of seeds. The seeds are harvested and dried.

Wheat is grown around the world. At the end of summer, the ripe seeds are harvested, using a combine harvester.

The maize plant produces a large seed head called a cob. It is ripe when the seeds are swollen.

Cereals include wheat, rice, barley, maize and rye. Wheat seeds may be milled or **ground** into a powder called flour. Flour is used to make bread, cakes and biscuits. Barley is used in beer making.

Maize, or corn, is used in breakfast cereals and other ready-made foods.

Rice plants are grown in flooded fields called paddies.

Healthy foods

People eat many types of plants, not just the staple foods. These plants include fruits, vegetables and nuts. They help to keep our bodies healthy because plant foods contain energy, protein, **vitamins** and **minerals**.

Vegetables, such as broccoli, beans and leeks contain vitamins and minerals that we need to keep us healthy.

Fruits contain natural sugar and many vitamins. Citrus fruits such as oranges and lemons are rich in vitamin C.

Every day, people need to eat small amounts of vitamins and minerals. If you do not eat a particular vitamin or mineral you can become ill. For example, not enough vitamin C can cause gum and skin diseases.

Nuts, such as these peanuts, are a good source of protein and fat. They are also important foods for vegetarians who do not eat meat.

Herbs and spices

Herbs and spices are used to flavour food to give it a better taste. They come from many different types of plants. Some are whole plants, and others are parts of plants. Leaves, flowers and seeds can all be used as herbs.

Chilli peppers taste hot. There are different kinds of chilli pepper and some are hotter than others.

Pepper is sprinkled over food to give it more taste. There are different types of pepper, including black, white and green. The peppers are dried berries.

There are lots of different spices. Cinnamon comes from the bark of the cinnamon tree. Vanilla comes from the pod of the vanilla orchid. Spices often have a hot taste, for example chilli, pepper and ginger. They make food taste sharper and more interesting.

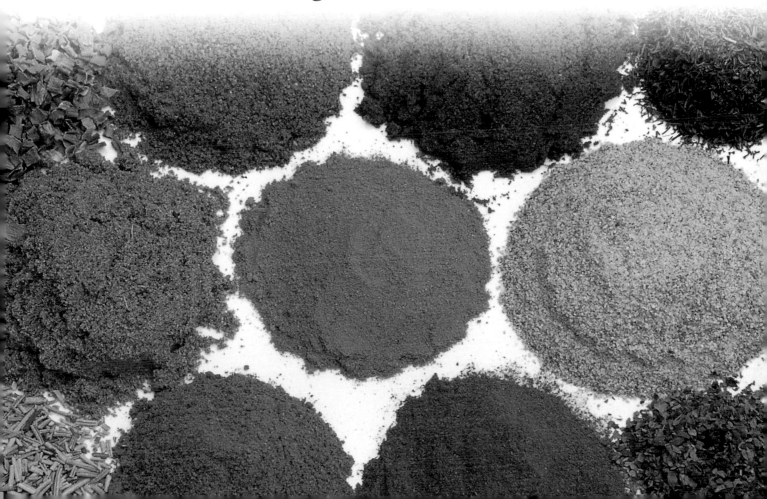

Colourful piles of dried herbs and spices. Herbs and spices may be sold fresh or dried. They can also he stored for use in the future.

Fibres

Fibres are long threads that have lots of different uses. Many important fibres come from plants, for example cotton, flax, jute, coconut and sisal.

Agave plants are grown to produce sisal which is used to make ropes, mats and rough flooring.

The cotton plant produces hairy seeds which are collected and made into cotton yarn. This is dyed and then spun into a cloth or fabric.

14

Cotton pickers remove the fluffy white seedheads from the cotton plants.

Flax is used to make a cloth called linen. Sisal comes from the agave plant and coir (koya) is taken from the outer covering of the coconut fruit. Sisal and coir are tough and hard-wearing fibres. They are made into doormats, carpet and ropes.

The brown fibres around the coconut are pulled away and used to weave mats and baskets.

Paper

People have written on paper for thousands of years. Paper can be made from several types of plants, including papyrus and reeds. Today, most paper is made from trees such as pine, spruce and eucalyptus (u-cal-ip-tus). The trees are cut down and the logs are taken to a **pulp mill**.

Logs are floated down a river to the pulp mill where the wood will be made into pulp.

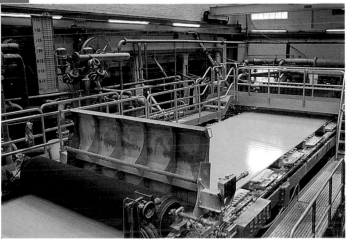

At the paper mill, the mixture of wood pulp, chemicals and water (left) is spread over a moving belt. Water drains out, leaving a sheet of paper which is squeezed flat and dried.

Here they are chopped into tiny bits. These are crushed to make a mushy pulp.

The pulp is taken to a paper mill where it is mixed with chemicals and water, and made into paper.

Papyrus is a large grass plant. The Ancient Egyptians used papyrus to make paper thousands of years ago. This was much thicker than the paper made today.

Oils

The seeds of many plants contain a lot of oil. Sunflowers,

Sunflowers are grown across the southern parts of Europe. Sunflower oil is used for cooking.

olives and soybeans are some examples. The seeds are harvested and then crushed to release the oil. Some of these oils can be used in foods. For example, sunflower oil is used in margarine, cooking oils and in many **processed foods**.

Palm oil comes from the fruits of the oil palm. It can be used as a cooking oil, made into a type of butter or used in a range of foods.

Some plant oils can be used as a fuel in cars, instead of petrol. A few plant oils are used to make medicines and **make-up.**

Fields of yellow oil seed rape is a common sight in early summer. The oil can be used in cooking and also as a fuel for cars and buses.

19

Trees for wood

Trees are large, tall plants. They have woody trunks which are very strong. The trunk is strong enough to hold up the branches. Wood is a very useful material. The wood from cone-bearing trees, such as the pine, is called softwood.

The tree trunks are taken to a **sawmill** where they are dried and cut into planks. Then they may be sprayed with a **preservative** so that they last longer.

Softwood is used in buildings and to make window frames and doors. The wood from slower growing trees such as teak, oak and beech is much harder. **Hardwood** is valuable because it lasts a long time.

Planks of wood have been used to support the roofs of these new houses.

*Hardwood is good for **carving** and can be used to make items such as wood sculptures.*

Growing more trees

When the trees are large enough, they are cut down and removed from the forest.

Each year, millions of trees are cut down for their wood, or timber. Trees are sometimes grown as a crop to provide a never-ending supply of timber.

Fast-growing trees such as pine and spruce are grown in large forests called **plantations**.

Young trees (front) have been planted to replace the old trees (back) that have been cut down.

The young tree seedlings are planted in rows. They grow quickly and within 30 to 40 years the trees are large enough to be harvested. Then the ground is cleared and new trees are planted.

Once the older trees are cut down, the ground is cleared and planted with tree seedlings. These will replace the cut trees.

Reeds and palms

Wood is not the only plant material that we use to build homes. Palm trees, such as coconut and date palms, grow in the tropical parts of the world. Palms have large, tough leaves called **fronds** which are ideal for making **thatched roofs.**

The coconut palm is very useful. We eat the flesh of coconuts, and the fibre in the nut is used to make coconut mats. The fronds of the plant are used as a building material.

Bundles of reeds are carefully fixed in place to make a thatched roof.

These roofs can keep the heaviest rain out. They are easy to repair if they are damaged in a storm. The reed is a large, grass-like plant that grows in damp ground. Bundles of reeds are used to make thatched roofs.

Reeds and palms are used to make baskets, mats and cane furniture

Medicine from plants

Lots of medicines are made from plants. One in every three medicines in use today has come from a plant. New **medicinal plants** are being discovered every year.

The drug digitalis comes from the foxglove. It is used to treat heart disease.

Juice from the leaves of the aloe vera plant can be rubbed into a wound to help it heal quickly.

Many **painkillers** are based on plant products. For example, aspirin was found in white willow, and morphine (a very powerful painkiller) comes from the opium poppy. Parts of some plants, such as the rosy periwinkle and the Pacific yew, have been used to treat some forms of **cancer**.

A medicine called morphine is made from the juice of the opium poppy.

Investigate!

Growing potatoes

Potatoes are easy to grow.

Plant the potatoes in an old bucket.

- Half fill an old bucket which has holes in the bottom with soil.

- Place 4 or 5 potatoes that have started to sprout on top and cover them with a little soil. Water the soil. Leave the bucket outside.

- After a few weeks, new shoots will appear above the soil. Add another layer of soil around the shoots. Keep adding soil as the shoots grow longer. Water regularly.

- In late summer the shoots will begin to die and you can dig up your potatoes.

Making dyes

> **Always ask an adult for help when using sharp objects such as knives.**

Many vegetables and fruits can be used as dyes, for example, onion skins, red cabbage, blackcurrants and beetroot.

- Chop up your chosen vegetable into very small pieces.

- Place the pieces in a saucepan with a piece of white cotton. Add enough water to cover.

• Heat the water for about 15 minutes, but don't let it boil. You may need to add extra water. Turn off the heat and leave to cool overnight.

• Wear rubber gloves, remove the cotton from the water and see if it has taken up the dye.

Chop the vegetables into small pieces

Making bowls

Newspaper can be used to make papier mâché bowls.

• Turn a small bowl upside down and smear Vaseline over it.

• Tear newspaper into strips about 2 cm wide by 8 cm long.

• Make a glue paste by mixing equal parts of flour and water together.

• Dip each strip in the paste and place it over the bowl. Cover the bowl in 5 layers of paper strips.

• Smooth the surface of the bowl and leave it to dry for 24 hours.

• Separate the papier mâché bowl from the real bowl and trim the top. Paint your bowl using acrylic paint.

Cover your bowl with newspaper strips making sure there are no gaps.

Glossary

cancer A disease in which the cells of part of the body divide without control and may form a growth or tumour.

carving To shape something by cutting.

cereal crops Grain-producing plants such as wheat, rice and maize. The crops are grown to produce a large amount of food.

crops Cultivated plants that are grown to produce a large amount of food.

energy The means or power for doing work.

diet The sort of foods that we usually eat.

fronds The leaves of ferns and palm trees.

ground Rubbed or crushed into a powder.

hardwood The wood of trees such as the oak, mahogany and teak.

herbs Plants with leaves, seeds and flowers which are used to flavour food.

make-up Powders, creams and lipsticks which are used to make the face more attractive.

medicinal plants Plants that can help to heal or cure illness.

minerals Substances such as iron or calcium that are needed in small quantities by the body in order to stay healthy.

painkillers Medicines that dull pain.

plantations Specially planted woods or forests with trees that are to be grown and then harvested.

preservative A substance which prevents wood from rotting.

processed foods Factory-made or manufactured foods such as crisps and biscuits.

pulp mill Where wood is made into pulp.

sawmill A place where logs are cut up into planks.

spices Plant substances that are added to food to give it a more lively or sharper taste.

staple foods The main part of the diet or food for many people. For example, wheat, rice and potatoes.

thatched roofs Plant material such as reeds which are used in bundles to make the roofs of some houses.

vitamins Substances that are needed in small amounts by the body to stay healthy, for example vitamin C.

31

Index